Reflections
Collection of poems and short notes

Reflections

Collection of poems and short notes

APARNA GURU

Black Eagle Books
2022

 Black Eagle Books
USA address:
7464 Wisdom Lane
Dublin, OH 43016

India address:
E/312, Trident Galaxy, Kalinga Nagar,
Bhubaneswar-751003, Odisha, India

E-mail: info@blackeaglebooks.org
Website: www.blackeaglebooks.org

First International Edition Published by
Black Eagle Books, 2022

REFLECTIONS
by **Aparna Guru**

Copyright © Aparna Guru

All rights reserved. No part of this publication may be reproduced, stored in a retrieval system, or transmitted, in any form or by any means, electronic, mechanical, photocopying, recording or otherwise without the prior permission of the publisher.

Cover & Inner art: Aparna Guru
Interior Design: Ezy's Publication

ISBN- 978-1-64560-303-0 (Paperback)
Library of Congress Control Number: 2022944476

Printed in the United States of America

The canvas is empty
White...Unblemished
The second page of my diary looks the same.

I lose myself in this emptiness for a moment
Putting aside the brush and the pen
And I paused...Until I felt...
Can I create something that would surpass the beauty of this moment
The essence of emptiness?

Else, I wouldn't be fair to these unsullied surfaces.

Contents

JOURNEY

Journey...13
Believe...14
Note (Never enough)...15
Soul...16
On the wheels of time...17
When in doubt...18
By the seaside...19
Note (Heart talks)...20

NIGHT

Story of the night...25
Note (Quiet)...27
One night...28
Moon...29
Krishna...30
Creatures of the night...31
Still...32

AUTUMN

Autumn road...35
Note (Fall)...37
Rain...38

QUEST

Quest of the wind...41
Happiness...44
Quest...45
Alone...46

Between craving & non-craving...47
Hope...49
Direction...50
Lost soul...51
Far away...52
Me...53

LOVE

Love...57
Note (Meditative)...58
Mystery...59
In love...60
Truth...61
For you...62
Escape...63
Love?...64
Note (Being free)...65
Note (Imperfect)...66

POETRY

Poetry...69
Wish...71
Note (Room)...72
Note (Routine)...73
Almost heaven...74
My mother's kitchen...75
Red house apartment...77
A walk in the woods...79
Sorrow...80
Empty...82
Mirror...83
Note (Determination)...84
Source...85

Dedicated to life that creates
the possibility to live, love and learn

A gift to my parents
Shri Saroj K. Guru & Smt. Nirupama Guru

Special thanks to my dear aunt Smt. Sneha Mishra for her support and encouragement in creating this book.

Journey

Journey

In a silent voyage of countless breaths & beyond
In a world of abundant beauty & calm
There awaits a destination
Where the thoughts cease to exist
Ideas dissolve
Remains there an ocean of knowledge...
An overflowing fountain of love & quest...

Truth is hidden somewhere
Beyond the eyes & the mind...
Death...A difficult test
Life...A prisoner of time

Love...The sole friend
Crossing the border between death & life
Life & Death…

Mind, a dictator of happenings
The plea of heart goes unheard...
Emotions, relations...All seem transient
Few footprints are still left in the past...

Life resumes its journey though
Like a flowing river changes its course...
River merges into the ocean
Life marching towards the unknown…

Believe

For all those filled with beauty & bliss
There is no room for remorse
No room for grief...

No room for despair
That let your spirit down...
No room for fear
No room for frown...

What life it would be
Where everything is bright and strong...
Would there be anything to reflect on?

And why do we reflect and what for...
Perhaps something within
Should know...Should grow...

Strong and becoming strong will never be the same
Not even the good and getting better...
You know...You said
There is room for growth in every sphere...

And we live this truth every single day
Still we pause and question ourselves
To get ready again for a deeper plunge...
Into the life's mystery
To its wisdom...

Never enough

Life is short...Dreams are big
Sometimes I feel, I must live many lives
to realize all my dreams
Or, what if...I could realize all of them
in just one life...
Will I stop dreaming then?
Will I stop longing for the eternity?

Soul

Soul...
A myth or the reality
Passport from the mortal to the immortality

Buried deep within the layers of
Belief and blind faith...
You reveal yourself
May be after death...

Who has seen you
And what are your aspirations...
If you are me
Then, stop being a stranger...

I feel...I imagine
But, then I'm a complicated mechanism
Body, brain and chemicals
I'm not sure...
If there is anything more?

But, not believing you
Invites more complications...
Life loses its meaning
Love...Its purpose

So, stay hidden
Till faith and reason meet...
Stay alive
Till we walk as one
On the path of eternity...

On the wheels of time

Quietly on the wheels of time
My days roll on...
The glittering gold dreams
On the silver paths of love...

Flowers, flowers everywhere
Wind wafts perfume divine...
Trees stretching there arms to the sky
To the lonely Lord in his distant shrine...

An ancient thirst that makes the rivers run
A quest that makes the wheels turn
Who knows, where the journey ends
The unknown purpose...
The unseen charioteer...

When in doubt

What am I...
A thought...An idea...A song?
I must be the poetry, you wrote that day
On an empty paper...

In a deep, dark night
When you felt that something was not just right
You were in doubt and a bit lost...
You felt like a stranger in a world that
You made...You owned...

So...You sat on the lap of a gently sailing cloud
Asked the wind, not to make any sound
You wanted calm...
And a deep silence fell over all
You were at ease with your pen & the paper...

Then...You wrote me
Picking up the words from the infinite set of words...
You wrote me in all the languages
As you were too modest to choose just one...

And you let me rhyme
With the lights of the blinking stars...
The rhythm of your beating heart...

Then a song was ready
That anyone can sing...
And for you to look back
In the old pages of your diary...
When the next time you feel lost
You will find yourself in me...

By the seaside

By the seaside
Watching the tides
Matched with my emotions...
The highs & The lows...

By the seaside
Looking at the horizon
Where the sea & the sky meet
One is deep...Other infinite
Both are beyond my comprehension...

By the seaside
When I realized...
That this is not a moment of quest
Not the moment to find myself back
But a moment to be nothing at all...
Hard to put it in words,
As if my spirit has found two wings...
And has set itself free...

Heart talks

Then the heart deciphered the hardest truth of the time
I belong to no one and nothing is mine
I go wherever my aspirations lead
I'm the wind...Wild and free
I see no heaven...No hell
Only a heart of love can hold me...

I'm beauty...I'm ocean quiet
I'm the river...An eternal flow of grace
I'm love, tear and thought...
I'm the truth...Invincible & Immense...

Night

Story of the night

The dim blue bulb
Night, quiet and dumb
Dreams are wild, untamed
Expedition of a lost nomad...

Many questions are asked
Many thoughts arise
Night never breaks its silence
Time seems to stand still...

An exchange of words for the thoughts
The communion of two empty souls
The repose of mind in the self
Like a bird flying to its nest...

On the empty pages of a diary
The night writes a story
And the silence, a song
Few pages talk about me
Few are left undone…

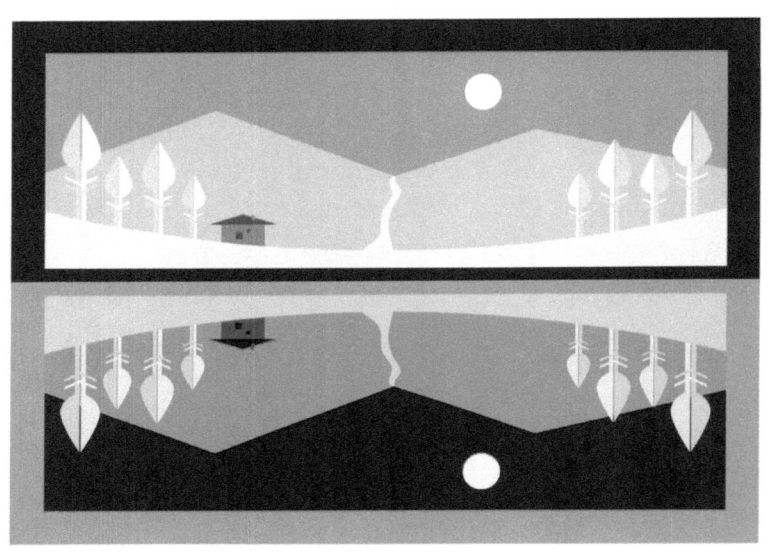

Quiet

A river of thoughts is flowing to the sea
To the sea...Down the hill
And none is there to hear
The song of the river
And none is there to feel
The joy of the sea
The night is still quiet...

One night

Serene and subtle
The silver moon sparkles
Amidst the tiny stars
Shining very far...

The whispering wind
Delicate & Divine
Sweeping away thoughts undesired
Feeling empty & full at the same hour...

Music, that the night plays
I find it hard to go to bed
The beauty and the peace within
The lingering moments of love...
Eyes laden with dreams unseen
And the silver moon sparkles...

Moon

Moon...Moon...
When You are with me
I leave everything behind
You are the mirror of my soul...

Life can't be simpler than this...
Moonlit night
And few lines of poetry...

Until I reach this moment
Whispering words
And you my dear friend
I don't feel quite right...

I sat on the floor
I love it, when the light is dim
And no one else is in the room
Just me, my poetry and the moon...

See...I thought of you
And words are flowing like a river
Can't fathom...
What kept them for so long
Moon...Moon...
You are the mirror of my soul...

Krishna

Moonlit path
Walking into the woods...
Lonely steps
Taking me to you...

And there you are
With your crescent smile...
Sitting on the throne of flowers
Playing the tune of night...

Creatures of the night

Listen to me Oh! Silver night
Don't want to sleep today
As you look so different
I've few words to say

Stars afar of mystic state
Stupor stature and distant gaze
With one eye closed and one opened
Peeping through their splendid souls

My eyes are getting heavy
And I'm drenched in the mist
Listen to me Oh! Silver night
I still don't want to sleep

White buds of night flowers,
Exudes the fragrance of love
I can't see a lover bee
Till the flowers wither

My hands are touching the flowers
But my Saree is stuck in the thorns
Listen to me Oh! Silver night
I can't go home...

Still

That winter night,
While I was trying hard to sleep...
Wearing my thin blanket
I felt no cold
But, sleep escaped...

Found myself fumbling in the dark
Sweet and bitter memories...
Well, sadness and regrets came first...

And it did not stop for long
So, finally I made my mind to create a song

And the words arrived from somewhere
May be from the mind... May be from my heart
Or may be from a land
Unknown and far...

So...I started to put them together
To make it my morning song
Didn't even realize
When the sleep came back
In that night poetry
I found my stillness...

Autumn

Autumn road

Tall trees...Purple leaves
Whispering wind passes by
Leaves rustle...
Bird flies
A little dream up in the sky...

A little fuss from the bush
A little squirrel scuttering by...

Far & Far...
There is not a single flower...Not a bee...Not the butterflies
The air is damp...
So is the street
So is my soul...

Restless steps on the autumn road...
Filled with leaves
The fallen dreams
The rising hope...
The autumn road...

Fall

There is life...There is death
Is there anything else left?
The leaves asked the trees...
Trees to the heaven...
Fall has come...
When would I rise again?

Rain

Rain...
Tears of the Sky
Pain of the Earth
When the lovers part...

Rain...
Joy of the blue hills
When the grey clouds embrace its peaks
Songs of praise...Drawing close
From the farmers of the distant fields...

Rain...
Pitter patter...
Roaring thunders...
Everyone runs for a cover...

Rain...
The little stream of mud...
Tears from the murky eyes
When the paper boat sunk...

Rain...
Drizzling down
Light wind...
Carrying the news of the clouds
The songs of the distant sky...

Quest

Quest of the wind

The age old thirst
Leads its way to me
Clearing the clouds away
It unfurls its wavy wings...

A touch so tender
A whisper like a wish
It makes the lost little tides breathe again
My stillness it steals...

But...The silence that is deep within
Is unbroken, untouched
In the hidden cavern of my heart
A strange loneliness lingers...

And the wind fails yet again
Its quest unfilled...

River

Do you my friend know?
Flowers bloom, when you come...

Happiness

Happiness…
A mirage on the bed of illusion or
A dumb distant star,
I see coming & going
Obligated to the constancy of its destiny…

Happiness…
A moment between two moments of emptiness
A quest in the desert of desires
That seems endless…

Yet…Each blind soul seeks
Every dreamer dreams
Through the silent murmur of prayers
The hardest way of sacrifice

Till…A day comes,
Shower of serenity flows
Deep into the heart of each seeker
And the sleepless eyes gleam
On the burning pyre of desire…

Quest

What the soul seeks
The unseen splendour of godliness
An unknown terrain to tread...

Silence...
How appealing...How deep...
Takes me with its tiny steps
A journey of quest
On the wheels of bliss...

I wonder...I wander
On a path made just for me...
Faith gives me strength
Love...My will...

Hard to imagine...
My own ignorance does not go away
And wisdom keeps coming in...
Day & night at the same hour
On the fathomless breast of time...

Alone

Like the wind...Like a bird
Open and out with wide wings
Voyaging in an endless aura...

Color me Oh! Waves of clouds
Break my dark monotony
I shrink to a starving soul
Why do you sail away from me?

I wander on an unknown path
Chasing something known
On the coarse breast of time
I leave my footprints on...

The world asks for my hands
Embraces me for a moment
The same destiny of pain and joy
Now, I feel no difference...

In a fathomless sea of white tides
I appear as a wave of hope
To fill in some fleeting purpose
Only my aspirations to be left alone...

Take me with you Oh! Distant friend
And break my solitude of ages
I'm longing for the forgotten rhythm
Playing beyond that sky...

Between craving & non-craving

What do I crave for...
Running in my red frock,
Untidy hair...Fifty paisa
I hear nothing...See none
To the candy shop...
Next moment,
I found myself lying on the middle of the road...
The rickshaw puller screamed
What are you up to kid...

What do I crave for...
Curious in the class
Sitting on the first row
Looking at the black board
Filled with letters of the last lesson
Some white chalks
Lying on the floor...
I picked one of those
And dusted the board clean...
I filled it with my dreams...

What do I crave for...
No, I never craved for love
Nor for the end of love...
It was just that
I met someone on a strange land
And then I watched him go...

What do I crave for…
Let me gather myself
As I'm scattered everywhere…
In the silence…With the crowd
With the stars far above the clouds
In the music & In colors
In the sweet fragrance of flowers
Fragments of my dreams…
Wherever I go…I see…
And in this moment
I've nothing left to crave for…

Hope

In the golden abyss of sunshine dreams
Lies the hope of an innocent world
Jewelled with laughter & joy
The unfailing flow of love & warmth...

The slow rising of the sleeping souls
Beneath the breast of a dubious culture
Doom & darkness melting down
In the quiet light of breaking dawn...

Lords of the human house
Break the shackle of partial faith...
Earth rejoices its promised freedom
Strength of her sons
Wisdom of her women...

Direction

From the point I started
And moved past those slender roads
Along the clumsy lanes
Seen through the fainted light...
The high walls of bricks
And the dark balconies...
Standing with hundreds of people,
Playing and laughing
Crawling on the dusty pathways...
Still stuck to the same place

I took my turn,
Leaving behind the people and their plays
Laughters, tears
And the annoying silence of the dead...
In my illusion of invention
Just to learn...
My destiny waited for me there,
Where I changed my direction...

Lost soul

What can I say?
I see my dumb face
With a smirk of quest...
I look at the world
A sea of unfathomed depth...

The silence of the graveyard
Swarm in my mind...
Seems like a desire long lost
Desperate and deprived...

I wander like a ghost
Unknown and unseen,
On the sparkling shades of nature
I see only my face reflecting...

I find my footprints
Left on the empty pathways,
I listen to my echoes
As no one else replies...

Am I a lone heart
Or a lost soul in the crowd of life?
What can I say?
I can no more imagine...

Far away

I wish I could go far away
From the murkiness of my dream...
The brief moments of reality
Waning in its own vanity...

I lounge in an armchair
Swinging my lazy limbs...
In the illusion of my ideas
Questioning a dream's obligation
And asking for its validity...

I wish I could go far away
From the doldrums of moments...
Dithering between hopes and dilemmas
In the cobwebs of actions and events...

Reality displayed in the dazzling daylight
Shining in a brilliance of joy...

Reality shrunk in its own prevalence
And fearing its fortitude
When a soul suffers and a life dies?

I wish I could go far away...

Me

Me...

What do I see?
The earth and the sky
And few colors in between,
Filling up a large empty canvas
That never really fills...
The rain comes for joy
And also comes the storms of sufferings...
Washing away all the hues
And leaving few little dots behind...

What do I hear?
Two lines of poetry sung by an aspiring soul
One line of beauty...One line of love...
And the noise of an imperfect note
Coming out of ignorance...Coming out of ego...

What do I feel?
Like a canvas hung since long
Colors have to be filled...
Like a song long written
Someone has to come and sing...
Like a mute body adding to the crowd of the world
Like an eternal soul
An ever burning fire...

Love

Love

Love...
Your innocence puzzles me sometimes
I don't understand your questioning eyes...

What do you ask from me...
In love heart is full
And mind is empty...

Meditative

Deep within my beating heart
Love's sweet song plays all the night
And my gaze fixed on the silver moon
I meditate on its beauty
As if lost in my lover's arm

One dream after another follows
I am full, yet… can't escape this moment's call
My eyes shine like two bright stars

Mystery

Have you my soul heard lately
Your heart is playing a different tune...
So enticing...So deep
It can almost dissolve you?

Have you felt its warm embrace
The strength of its closeness...
When the last time you shut your eyes
And the first time you opened them?

What is it?
That is so much of your own
And still so hard to comprehend...
You struggle to get hold of it
And it hides its face...

Only a faint murmur, a swift glance &
a fleeting moment of solitude...
And it escapes...Yet again
Not to be bothered...Not to be understood

In love

Love kills...
Poetry resurrects...
The sweet poison of longing
The old wine of wisdom
I drink all at once
Doesn't matter how good or bad it is...
There is something about the way
I love...I live...

Truth

Who knows, what is Truth
How true is my aspiration?
How true is my soul?

Each time amidst my desires
I am left alone
Each time I find myself
Imprisoned in a house of emotion

Never knew what it takes
To live a life full of grace

Each time I climb those steps of inspiration
Each time I try to hide my desperation
Love finds me back
Embraces me for a moment
Then disappears in the waves of time
Leaving me behind with my incomplete truth
My partial being...

For you...

Conquering heart...
Ah! I'm such a failure in that
I'm pretty, I speak less & I don't pretend...

And I won't lie to steal your soul
Even if I want it the most...

Well...For the rest of the world
I'm asked to stay patient...
Loving without expectations
And to be kindest to the cruel...

Not so easy all the time
I bleed again before the old wound heals...

Still I mange to find time for you...
For you to remind me
I do this all for the good...

Escape

Flowing with the wind
Flowing with the stream
Flowing with my thoughts...
Pink sky...Purple clouds...Emerald dreams...

White feathers on
Flying high...
As far as I may...
Never looking back...

Moist eyes...Misty air...
My soul is still wet
Heart aches...
Never looking back...

Love?

And I thought again
Why did I fall in love?
The greatest desire
Or simply a reason to suffer?

The struggle between
The reasons and the beyond
Justifiable or Inevitable
Love is tender
And yet so powerful...

Love imagines
Love creates...
Love unites
Love liberates...

And love stays...
Just the way it was...Just the way it is...
While we move on
Love lingers for the eternity...

Being free

Few little words...
If left unspoken...Will lose their meaning of being
Urging me to unleash them
As if a river stopped on its way to the ocean by a dam
Pushing it with all its might
To break it apart...
So, is the language of my heart...
And those few little words...

I broke those walls
And set them free...

Imperfect

You are so undone...
Careless strokes,
Broken curves...
And what made me stop?
Your innocence
Simply fills everything up.

Poetry

Poetry

Poetry...
The song of solitude
A query of the heart
Flight of the mind
A journey of words...

Few lines of inner quest...
A voice in depth...

Or is it the silence of my soul?
Striving to be known...

Poetry...
A picture long drawn...
Seeking expression...

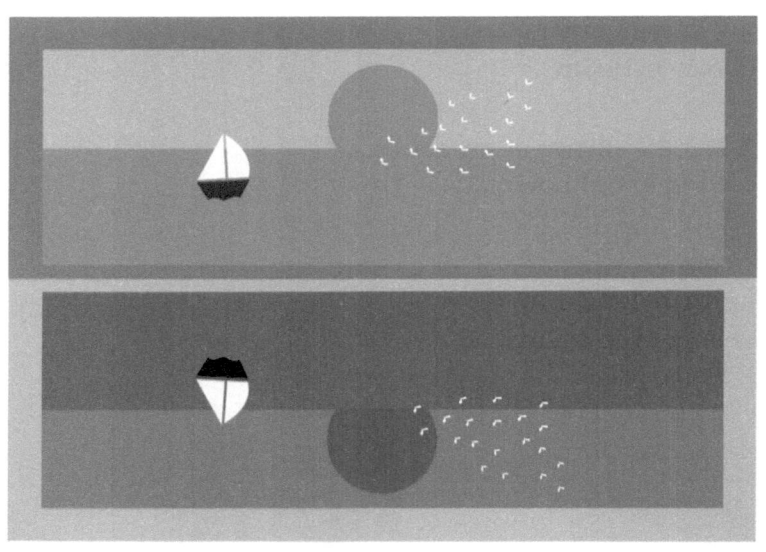

Wish

A wish is like a ripple
On the ocean of silence...
Like the waves of wind
Playing with a burning flame...

I gaze at you...
Oh! Divine flame
And let the hours pass by...
May my ignorant thoughts
Would not bring the waves of change...

For the new may arrive
From the spheres of the sincerest wishes...
For the new may arrive
From the realms of wisdom & grace...

Room

It is just another day...
Same room,usual stuffs
Nothing changed
But a bit of thought...

And arrays of colors are splashed on the walls...

The usual is crumpled, bent, beautified
Or just left untouched in the corner...
Pile of old books
And my new fairy doll...

Routine

I've a small cottage...By the blue lake
Close to the Daffodil hill

In the morning...
I tend to the plants...Talk to the flowers
And watch the floating Dandelions in the air

At night...
I weave dreams...By the silver stream
And travel far...
To the moon...To the sparkling stars

Almost heaven

The misty morning air
The faint light seen through the blinds
Lingering under the lids of sleep
My dreams of last night...

The scent of roses
I feel fresh & new
Leaving the bed behind
I stroll on the green grass barefoot
Feeling the dampness warming my soul...

Sun, smiling like an infant...Innocent & sweet
Flowers blooming, beaming with joy & beauty...

Birds flying like a group of dancing ballet...
Humming to some heavenly rhythm
Playing in the sky...

A quick splash of cold water on my face...
On a mute form of flesh & blood
Rain of life & grace...

The burning candles
For the half known Lord...
Few words of love
Some secret murmur...
And a prayer in silence
Thanking him for a beautiful day...

My mother's kitchen

I think of my mother's kitchen...
Something very much known
But never tried to explain...

My mother's kitchen
Or the destiny of art...
A brush of red chili
A touch of turmeric on its walls...

I think of my mother's kitchen
Like a store house of my fancy...
Pepper, salt, sugar and spices
I can find anything
But not the chocolate cookies...

My mother's kitchen
Or a complex riddle of jars...
I fumble and startle
As she takes her afternoon nap...

I think of my mother's kitchen
In a charming sunlit morning...
When the warm smoke swirls out
Through the rusted chimney...

The rice boils in the silver pot
The dal simmers in the cooker...
The kitchen fills up
In a warm aroma of flavors...

My mother's kitchen
Is very personal to her...
She never lets me play around
Not with the food...Not with the jars...

Red house apartment

On the sprawling lap of time
Lay down an apartment
With broken limbs
And wounded dreams...
Deep under the debris of bricks
Searching for his shadow
And hiding his anguish...

Red house apartment
Standing high along the highway
And kissing the sky with confidence...
He looks like a prince with a crown
When the silver clouds pass by...

Red house apartment
Or an epitome of life
Housing thousands of thoughts
And living hundred of dreams...

Red house apartment
A treasure of memories
A measure of moments...
With each person coming and leaving
Neither has he asked
Nor he regrets...

Red house apartment
Observes quietly
The ballet of happiness

And the cries of worries
The crowd of colors
And the laughter of babies...

Red house apartment
A symbol of silence...
Amalgamation of ideas
In a mist of noise...

Red house apartment
The dream house for many
Is lying under his remains today,
Amassing the fragments of his scattered dreams...
That he saw once but could not live...
Closing his eyes in the haze of despair
Deep under the debris of broken bricks...

A walk in the woods

That day... While walking past the whispering woods
Gathering the fallen foliage of wisdom
Listening to the soft voices
Of the known and the unknown...
The buzzing bees
And the lost tune of the soul...

A glimpse at the shadows on the sun scattered soil
The peek a boo of the form with the formless...

The vast veil of heaven over the earth
The crimson and yellow of the sun
The glittering silver of the moon and the stars...

The flowing blue stream on the forest floor
The little leaves sailing afar
The scent of damp soil
When the wet wind waves past...

The magic note of hanging chimes
And the sweet murmuring of some ancient tone
The night dance of forest folks
The smoky air is whirling up...

Sorrow

No, I never wanted to know
What did that create sorrow?
Pains that are clasped in the bosom
And fears that overflow the eyes...
I behold it wherever I go
The deep scar of wound never heals...

Under the white sheet of happiness
The dark sorrows peep...
Looking hither and thither
For someone to come and reveal...

A tear washed face pop up
After each heartfelt laugh,
Like a sleeping baby cries
When oust from its mother's lap
The taunt of pain
And the toll of sufferings
The helpless people
And hopeless dreams...

Still, they breathe and live
As pleasure is never without pain,
How could only pain be?

So, let the pain never scare
Let not hold only to despair
Happiness is just a night away
For a heart of hope...A spirit of courage...

Empty

Emptiness...
I sought you the other day
Amidst my crowding thoughts
Along the walkway...Stretching like a snake
Swallowing me deep into the depth of uncertainty...

I thought of being in your arms...
And taking a long nap
And waking up to the tune of something sweet & warm...

Something happens...
Each time I try to touch you in the deep cavern of my heart
Love, hope, eternity, respite
Whatever you name it...
I'm full
When I'm empty...

Mirror

Treasured in the heart of glass
Still opaque your dreams are
What is behind that beaming body
Asked her innocent eyes?

Blushed the shiny sculpture
Soft words...Gentle approach

A handful of your scattered thoughts
And the diversity of your gestures...

The songs that you sing before me
The names that you scribble on my dusty surface...
The essence of your fragrant figure
The colors that make your face...

Or should I remind...The story of the last night

Tears rolling down your cheeks,
Washed away the hues you wore...
The melting colors painted me
My heart is still hurt...

You yelled at me and whined,
I can never forget the look of your misty eyes...

Her innocent eyes smiled with a spark,
As a quiet lake with tiny stars
She opened a box of trinkets
And drew a pink smile on the mirror's face...

Determination

I was reading from the book of life
And each chapter seemed to be a dream half-lived
An incomplete...A partial truth

But, now I've no time to look back & reflect
The book is still in my hands
And has to be read the proper way till the end...

No missing letters...No half-lived dreams
Before I lose myself
In the light of the deep dreamless sleep...

Source

Did I ever exist...Before I came to this world?
And who knows their histories
Beyond their memories
Does the source of things lie in the past?

I wanted to take a deeper dive
But I needed to keep up with the present time
I just could not move any further
Asked myself...Is there something left to be discovered?

Is something really calling me back...
Something undone...Needs to be mended
Something unreached...Waiting to be touched?

And what sheds light on the past
And what is looking for the answers?

Life has opened its eyes
But time keeps its secrets behind...

And what lies ahead?
Unseen & Unknown...
Why it can't be just left alone?

Time has a book to keep
But I've only got fleeting memories
And what should I aspire for?
For I believe in love
We always find each other...

And what greater truth is there to be known
And what greater beauty is yet to be discovered?

Black Eagle Books

www.blackeaglebooks.org
info@blackeaglebooks.org

Black Eagle Books, an independent publisher, was founded as a nonprofit organization in April, 2019. It is our mission to connect and engage the Indian diaspora and the world at large with the best of works of world literature published on a collaborative platform, with special emphasis on foregrounding Contemporary Classics and New Writing.

www.ingramcontent.com/pod-product-compliance
Lightning Source LLC
Chambersburg PA
CBHW020545080526
44583CB00013B/1011